American Realist Painters
Nick Monks

Bluebell Publishing

By the Same Author:

Poetry

By The Canal (Masque Publishing)
Winter Trees
Cities Like Jerusalem
Narratives
Homes
The Love Songs of James Dyer
Gardening
Greek Olympian Myth
Snow
England's of the Mind
Imaginary Friends
Footprints (the Disparate)

Plays

Le Conquet (The Refugees)

Short Stories

Aegean Islands

Title page

American Realist Paintings- Nick Monks

Published October 2019

Printed by Lulu October 2019

www.lulu.com

ISBN: 978-0-9955203-01

For Amanda, Karl, Saskia

Acknowledgments: The Art Institute of Chicago deemed not to reply to my e-mail requesting to insert a copy of Edward Hopper- Nighthawks in this book.

Contents

American Realist Painters

Edward Hopper- Nighthawks

The interior is green like a farm pond
The wood cherry brown
Red brick houses along the street habitations

Why are they/we so alone?
Nearly as alone as married couples with three children-
But not quite
As the man at a football match
As one in the undifferentiated crowd

What do these four people dream of?
Chevrolets?
White wood boarded houses?
The final deal that makes them- rich?
Becoming the family in glossy commercial adverts?

Ministered to by a barman

Is the alone man's wife waiting in a downtown apartment?
"Another bourbon for the road" says Frank
Before he goes out into the empty night

I guess they have a living to make
Respectable in their way
We are invited to view them in their neon green fish tank

And the city murmurs and babbles and they are alone and small

So, its late in downtown New York
Are they nursing their dreams in a down- town city diner?

Do they have hope?

Each conforms to his/her place in the diner
It's as if the cosmos can't fit them in
Or has too much space to notice.

George Bellows-The Lone Tenement

We stand beneath the bridge

We are not part of New York
Light cascades here to
And what we/they are building is unfinished

When it is finished, the litter men will come-
Clean us away
And business- men will make money in the new tenement

The river is a silver sash of hope
Its dark under the bridge
Stick ants in the urban undergrowth

The darkened figures, there for eight months
Then disappeared
The new gleaming tenement
The new passers -by and workers in the neon city.

Childe Hassam-The Avenue in the Rain- (flags series)

Blue gold rain, New York
What more could you ask

Detroit ghost city, deprivation
The rich escape to Martha's Vineyard

We built Chicago on the bones of the dead

Me I sit within and paint snow in New York
As it is decided in chaos who will win and who not

Seven figures walk through a cathedral of silver blue

Cradled in the rain the patriotic flags are beautiful
Unfurling fluttering like snow, in the shimmering blue city.

John Singer Sargent-Rosina- (depicting Rosina Ferrara)

White blouse, pink skirt

She looks back
Smiles
Jet black done up hair

Carrying a string of onions
She embraces enchantment for us

Her smile contains a thousand rivers-
Is bridgeless

Then I imagine she turns and walks away

Carrying jouissance with her

What sublimity to catch the moments she made
In a painting.

James Whistler- Arrangement in Grey and Black No 1 (The Mother)

You view her askance
All sideways

But she is full like a Rousseau Forest
The tempest ace ness of a farm lullaby
The first reading of the Pauline epistles

She is both diminutive and realized
Her world is glance less inner meditation

At home in grey, black, white
She does not need red, orange, green, blue
She is outside of all/ inside

Mona Lisa in Connecticut
Mary Magdalene
Danu and the Maid de Orleans

All know her

Hail hallelujah

The bears and goshawks and otters dance
While she sits sideways. More wordless than New York or
Chicago or Detroit or Pittsburgh.

Mary Cassatt- Woman Sewing

The room is a bathosphere
Besieged by storm water, seaweed and boulders

There a lady sews cloth. Or seals a letter
Or cherished moments with a child

Intent in dark dress with lace collar
A bunch of blue flowers in a vase
Dull yellow wallpaper

And the incantations of craft and sewing
Are a magical home ordered interior
An inward meditation. The city's teeming elsewhere.

Thomas Eakins- Agnew Clinic

The men in the amphitheatre seats confer
Witness become scientific and puritanically practical

Its serious

The scalpel is immonde

Imagine red lipstick, Chanel perfume and clamps and blood
drainage tube
It may not get messy, we are avid pioneers

And the light is streaming on the surgeons
The onlooker's medical students learn their career paths.
We are intent. Pointedly curious and engrossed.

Not chatter/gossip/ other types of noise

Can you here the oceans tide. Quantified, measured, mapped.

James Whistler- Nocturne: Blue and Gold (Old Battersea Bridge)

The light saturates
Breaths
Sweats
A kiss

For the smog, sexually blue

This light is dreaming
A nose flattened against a city door

Its ok

We'll build everywhere
Until the blue light sanctifies the river Thames, Battersea
Bridge
And Byzantium, Babylon, Alexandria

Breathe.

Grant Woods- American Gothic

I came from the Netherlands
On a ship of mermaid's songs

We are godly
Steadfast
Hard working
Debauchery- less

We are the good ghosts
Pure as wool and milled flour

We read the gospels at cheap but sturdy
Plain wooden tables. Seriously intent

The mermaid's harps stay with us

Through the masts cables the songs vibrated
We merely build a new land into a kingdom.

Everett Shinn- Signs of Spring

In green coat
Umbrella accosted by wind and rain
Face turned

At one with the elements
Yet divine

This is Ravels- Bolero
Gershwin's- Rhapsody in Blue
Stravinsky's- Rights of Spring

She has tamed a city
Made it blush silver.

Raphael Soyer- City Children

Two women
One holding a baby
One woman in red skirt
Holding a black child's hand
The other child occupied with his hand

The divine beautiful democracy of poverty

In a grubby dark street
Before a door
The door exists as a retreat to go back into

Unseen
Uncharted by social scientists in universities

Blood red skirt
Blue cosmos jumper
One more baby carried in harness

Like millions
Charted by Jack London, John Updike,
Muriel Rukeyser

Their reconnoitre revealed little

The interior is a type of prison
A basic celebration of sheer elan.

Isabel Bishop- People Walking

The woman goes left
The woman goes right
Others in the background walk
In directions

All bathed in a societal sea of red
A cathedral of crowdism
Of individuation

The light so magnificent
Through the stained- glass sky
Hop- scotch for gods and goddesses.

George Luks- The Ledge

Green sea
Tumultuous deep
Primeval force

Here I would stand with my father
Here I would stand alone
Throw stones into the green sea

Which takes the gift and reply's with waves
The fluid sea harp, undaunted.

Raphael Soyer- Passerby

The mannequin's heads are lifeless
And she
Anxious walking home from work
The sidewalks are alien
And she is hurried
A hat a done up, coat collar against the cold

A husband sits in a flat lounge, smokes a woodbine

And upon her arrival
The city cascades into cello and clarinet snow drifts

And she's walking through the mined corridors of tall steel
scrapers

Another figure in the crowd hurrying home.

Winslow Homer- Blown Away

Two brothers in a boat
The white sail against silver sea

Soon it will be pitch black
Moon stars waves murmuring to each other
The salt sharp, blissful ecstatic shipwreck

But oh- the silver sea, the silver sky, the white sail
The stories we made to be told and re told.

Thomas Pollock Anshutz- The Ironworkers' Noontime

We live in grime
There are millions of us
Without legal rights or citizens charter

We are physicality flesh
The women like us
As we don't think

Made redundant by optic fiber and silicon chip

Making iron
Making us like iron
Baked dry in the noon sun.

John Singer Sargent- Cashmere

They could be Paul on the Damascus road
After the vision that is
Pioneer puritans walking to a wedding
Draped in cashmere shawls
The anchorage of Boston art
The idyll of Seattle woods
The factories of Detroit

More beautiful than leopards or snow terns
I cannot say anything else.

William Merritt Chase- Portrait of a Gentleman

One son two daughters
Works for a bank
Slipping towards old age
The chin raised
Light on the hard- working face
All else black

His illuminated steadfast face
Forging a new world
Indomitable and trepid

Before he slips back into the dark
Remembered in an art gallery.

James Whistler-Grey Note- Mouth of the Thames

Clouds buoyant
A painting hemmed in by gold
Two silhouettes of yachts
On the silver water
One dark yacht. One light

Sailing away into the vast
Foretold north- sea
Which is sequestered- weighed down with gold on- silver.

www.ingramcontent.com/pod-product-compliance
Lightning Source LLC
Chambersburg PA
CBHW021922040426
42448CB00007B/874